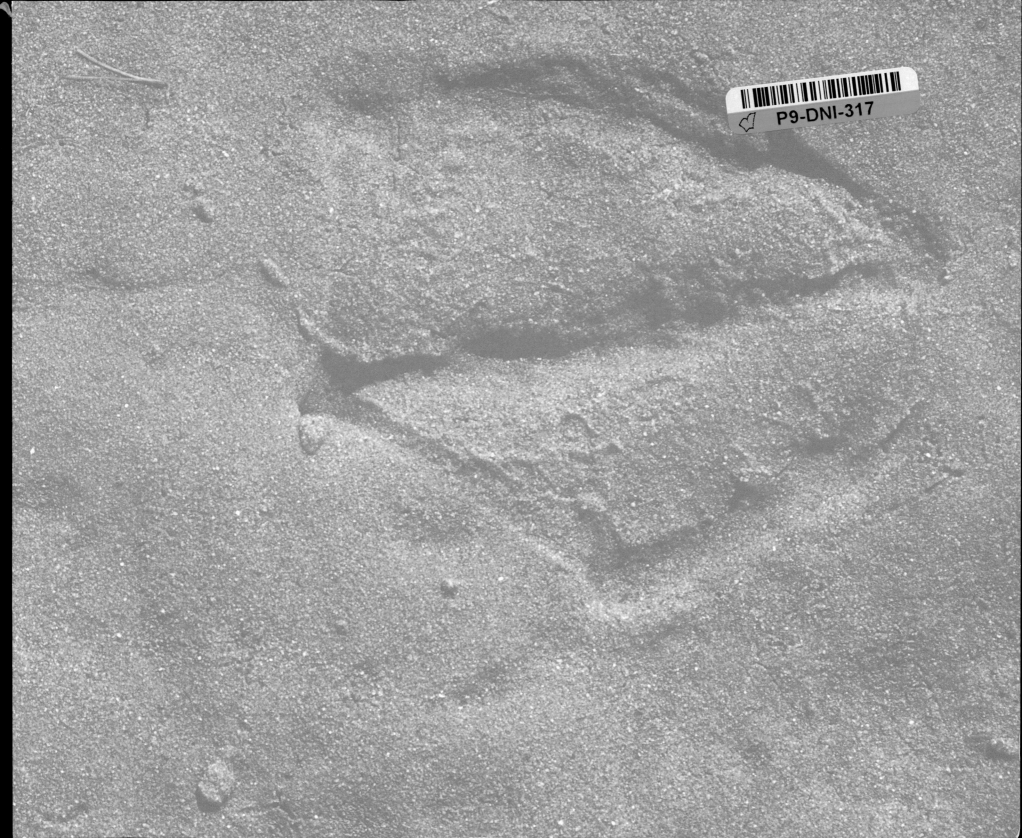

Project UltraSwan

written and photographed by Elinor Osborn

HOUGHTON MIFFLIN COMPANY · BOSTON 2002

www.houghtonmifflinbooks.com

The text of this book is set in Weiss and Tema Cantante.
Endpapers: Life-size trumpeter swan tracks.
Maps on pp. 31, 32, 52, and 58 by Jerry Malone
Design by Lynne Yeamans

Library of Congress Cataloging-in-Publication Data

Osborn, Elinor.
Project UltraSwan / Elinor Osborn.
p. cm. — (Scientists in the field ; 6)
Summary: Describes the life of large trumpeter swans, how they nearly became
extinct, and efforts to help them relearn migration routes and to reintroduce them to
the eastern United States.
ISBN 0-618-14528-1 (hardcover)
1. Trumpeter swan—Juvenile literature. [1. Trumpeter swan. 2. Swans.]
I. Title. II. Series.
QL696.A52 O82 2002
598.4′184—dc21
2002000223

Printed in Singapore
TWP 10 9 8 7 6 5 4 3 2 1

For trumpeter swans.
May your great wings grace
our eastern skies again.

Flying Lessons

It sounds like an overgrown mosquito.

But in the dim light just before sunrise, you can see that it's a tiny airplane, flying low, coming toward you. It's much too cold for mosquitoes anyway. This is October in western New York State, and you shiver in the frosty air.

You are standing on a small hill, watching the plane circle. Van headlights bounce along on the rough field below, and you strain to see what is happening. As the headlights stop, the plane circles again, touching down by the van. Then, someone, crouching out of sight, throws open the gate on a small trailer hitched to the van. Five large, pale gray birds scramble out, enormous wings flapping hard—hurrying to follow the plane into the air.

These are young trumpeter swans, just four months old, up early for their flying lessons. When full grown, they will turn shining white and will be the largest waterfowl in North America, in fact, the largest in the world. (Of the flying birds, only the Eurasian great bustard and the African kori bustard are heavier.) An adult male trumpeter can stand face to face with an eight-year-old child. And if you asked the trumpeter to stand in a single-car garage doorway, his spread wings would reach across the eight-foot opening. He needs that

5

broad a wingspan to lift his thirty pounds off the ground. Trumpeter swans are the largest birds to migrate long distances. Some small birds nearly double their weight in fat to fuel up before migrating thousands of miles. Swans can't do that. Add any more weight, and their wings wouldn't lift them. Even with normal weight, they need to run a bit before they can lift off. Lighter birds like robins can make a quick getaway, flying almost straight up.

As soon as these young swans learn to fly well, their next lesson will be learning a migration route. They are students in the second year of the Trumpeter Swan Migration Project—a scientific project investigating whether humans can teach trumpeter swans to migrate again after they disappeared from the eastern part of North America. What caused the disappearance? By 1900, hunters had shot them all. Only a few in the West survived.

Historical records show that, in summer, trumpeter swans lived on lakes and ponds

in forests and prairies over most of North America. They wintered on rivers and seacoasts in what is now the southern United States. For thousands of years, swan parents taught their youngsters a migration route by leading them to their wintering area and back. Scientists don't know why swans and geese must learn their routes while other birds hatch with instincts telling them to migrate in the correct direction. For example, the shorebirds that you see on Atlantic beaches from July into August are adult birds, migrating south three to six weeks ahead of their youngsters. The young shorebirds are left to navigate on their own—for thousands of miles!

RIGHT: *Gavin is ready to take off in the trike.*

With the shooting of the last trumpeter swan east of the Mississippi River, no swans were left there to remember the migration routes. Now only humans know those routes. And to teach the swans the routes again, humans must lead them in the air.

The aircraft the birds are rushing to follow this morning looks like a three-wheeled go-cart (pilots call it a "trike") with a big propeller in back, all suspended under a hang glider wing. A trapezelike bar steers it. It's called an ultralight. And it is—when you compare its 254 pounds with a single-engine airplane's more than 2,000 pounds. Because these swans fly with an ultralight, project leaders named them UltraSwans.

Their teacher, Gavin Shire, pilots the yellow ultralight this morning. He is a biologist playing the role of a parent swan teaching the youngsters to follow him in the air. Another pilot, Brooke Penny-packer, acts as an aerial cowboy. He rounds up wayward UltraSwans and herds them back to Gavin's wingtips.

Gavin has been fascinated with birds and animals since he was a teenager growing up in England. It was no surprise when he chose to study zoology in college. Gavin's eyes light up as he remembers riding the bus home for one school vacation. "I looked out, going along at forty-five miles an hour, and there was a bird, a small falcon, flying dead-level with the bus window. It must have lasted all of five seconds, but that got me interested in bird flight."

After graduating, Gavin worked with endangered falcons, next, with owls. Then, as a biologist with Environmental Studies at Airlie, a research institute in Virginia, he was asked to take care of a flock of Canada geese. Why would a flock of geese need a caretaker? These were special geese—pioneers in an experiment. Canadian Bill Lishman, a sculptor and pilot, was teaching them a migration route.

In his book *Father Goose*, Bill recounts how he had dreamed of flying since he was eight years old. As an adult that dream broadened to include flying with birds. Bill experimented with a hang glider, even adding a motor. He rebuilt the hang glider many times, transforming it into a real, though tiny, airplane. During one of his early-morning flights, a flock of wild ducks suddenly surrounded Bill, accepting him as another bird. It was such a remarkable experience that he became obsessed. He was determined to fly with birds again.

When Bill heard of a man training Canada geese to follow a motorboat, he wondered if he could train geese to follow his aircraft. It worked. A human could fly with birds!

OPPOSITE: *Brooke follows in another trike to herd wandering swans back to Gavin's wingtips.*
ABOVE: *Bill Lishman* (right) *found an enthusiastic supporter for his goose migration project in Dr. William "Bill" Sladen* (left), *who is now the director of the Trumpeter Swan Migration Project.* © Gavin G. Shire

9

One fall Bill flew a group of geese from Canada to Virginia, where Gavin took care of them for the winter. As part of Gavin's "goose-sitting" salary, Bill offered to teach him to fly an ultralight. But Gavin wasn't ready for that. He didn't even like riding in airplanes. Gavin said he'd think about it. He thought for a long time—a year—but finally he agreed. First he learned to fly the trike. Then he was ready to train geese to fly. Gavin says, "I still hate flying on the big commercial planes, but I love to fly in that trike—go figure. Maybe it has something to do with being in control. I had watched bird behavior on the ground, and the idea of experiencing that in the air was irresistible. Prior to Bill Lishman's work with geese, no one had ever studied bird behavior in the air. Taking science that one step further appeals to me."

Gavin helped fly Bill's third goose migration. Gavin's trike led one flock and a second trike led another flock. Along the way Gavin looked back to see the other flock joining his own, sixty-two birds forming a line off his right wing. "What an incredible sight! The line stretched so far back I couldn't even see the birds at the end."

Bill's experiment led scientists to believe they might be able to teach trumpeter swans to migrate too. But Gavin and Brooke wondered if it would be possible to fly ultra-lights with swans. Trumpeters are so much heavier and so much more powerful than geese. Would their great flapping wings create such air turbulence that the pilots wouldn't be able to control their aircraft? No one had tried flying ultralights and swans together. As it turned out, Gavin felt turbulence only when a swan flew in front of the wing. Even so, he didn't lose control.

Flying in the ultralight on this cold October training day Gavin shivers even while wearing three pairs of gloves and five layers of clothing, including insulated coveralls. The UltraSwans are warm, though! Their feathers are so dense they can tolerate temperatures as

OPPOSITE, LEFT: *A bird has different kinds of feathers. The barbules on the flight and contour feathers hook together so that no air leaks through.*
OPPOSITE, RIGHT: *Preening zips up each feather, leaving no holes.* © Gavin G. Shire

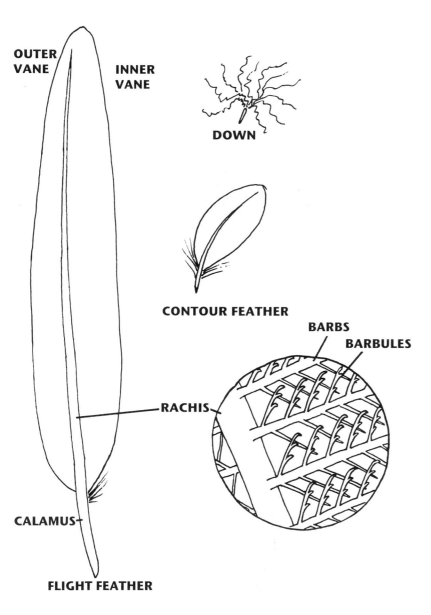

OUTER VANE

INNER VANE

DOWN

CONTOUR FEATHER

BARBS

BARBULES

RACHIS

CALAMUS

FLIGHT FEATHER

RIGHT: *A trumpeter spreads oil from the uropygial gland.*

BELOW: *Swans like to fly off the ultralight's wingtips. It's easier there. A cushion of air gives them a lift.*

low as 20 degrees below zero Fahrenheit. Just as the puffy lining of a parka traps warm air next to a human's body, a swan's two-inch-thick layer of fuzzy down feathers traps the warmth coming from its body. Instead of a nylon shell, a swan grows long, firm feathers; these contour feathers form a windproof "coat" over the down. To keep its thousands of feathers in good condition, a swan spends up to six hours a day preening. It pulls the contour and flight (wing) feathers through its bill to zip together the feather barbules, which have hooks so tiny you need a microscope to see them. Swans nibble smaller feathers into place. While preening, a swan applies a waterproof coat with oil from the uropygial (your-oh-PIJ-ee-al) gland at the base of the tail. The bill and the back of the head serve as spreaders. A long neck with more than three times as many vertebrae as a giraffe's makes the job easy.

Why do Gavin and Brooke choose the coldest part of the day, the early morning, for flying? Winds are usually calm then. In gusty wind steering the aircraft becomes difficult. Swans, though, have a delicate feel for wind shifts. Their flexible wings not only have elbow and wrist joints but muscle control of each flight feather as well.

When Glory, swan number 18, feels a gust, he reacts instantly, flying straight without a hitch. Ultralight pilots react much more slowly. It figures. Birds have millions of years of flying practice, but humans have just over a hundred.

The UltraSwans enjoy flying close to the trike's wingtip. That's where they catch an easy ride—an invisible cushion of lift. In that spot, all that's needed is a shallow flick of the wingtips, while trumpeters flying farther back must pump their wings much harder. Gavin has observed the swans pecking one another's tails—fighting for that treasured spot.

On each training day, as Gavin flew with the UltraSwans, he anxiously wondered about the migration to come. Would the swans follow him 320 miles to the Chesapeake Bay?

The Swans Are Missing

In the fall, anywhere in the Northeast, if you look up into the blue sky, you can see long, wavering Vs of Canada geese flapping their way south. Imagine how it must have been to see trumpeter swans, three times the size of Canada geese, flying in lines across the sea of blue sky, glistening white in the sun.

Except for a few isolated sightings, trumpeter swans were last reported along the Atlantic coast more than 200 years ago. It is estimated that when the first colonists came to North America in the early 1600s, one hundred thousand trumpeters wintered on the Atlantic coast from the Chesapeake Bay south to Florida.

Especially in the winter, swans provided much-needed food for the earliest colonists. The large, shining white targets were easy to shoot out of the sky. Except for man and grizzly bears, healthy adult swans have no other predators. Coyotes, eagles, mink, snapping turtles, and owls try to catch young swans, called cygnets, but at great risk. With their powerful wings parent swans can kill a dog-sized animal.

As pioneers moved inland they entered the swans' breeding areas. There, swans were even easier to hunt. For a month each

summer adult swans are grounded as they molt (lose and regrow) their flight feathers. Cygnets are grounded too, until they begin to learn to fly at about four months old.

As eastern cities grew in population, the demand for meat grew as well. No laws prohibited shooting birds, and market hunters, as they were called, shot all kinds of wild birds—by the thousands. They sold swan meat and eggs in the American colonies. About 1769 the Hudson's Bay Company, known for their fur trade in western North America, began shipping swan skins—feathers attached—to England. There, wealthy people who wanted to be stylish wore robes made of the skins with their cascading white feathers. Skins with tiny inner down feathers made soft powder puffs. Larger feathers decorated ladies' hats in both England and America.

We almost lost them. In 1912 an ornithologist (bird scientist) writing about the trumpeter swan said, "Its total extinction is now only a matter of years." None could be found east of the Mississippi River. In the West, there were only two known nestings between 1900 and 1912—one in Alaska and one in Montana.

Recently, scientists studying trumpeter swan fossils from Oregon, Illinois, and Florida found evidence of just how ancient these birds are. The fossils date back 12,000 years. However, in the short space of three hundred years humans had nearly exterminated these majestic birds.

Then, good news! In 1919 two trumpeter swan families were found nesting in Yellowstone National Park. A new law, the Migratory Bird Treaty of 1918, signed by the United States and Canada, protected them from hunters. Left alone, the trumpeters in the Yellowstone area increased to sixty-nine birds by 1932.

There was more good news. In 1955 a biologist discovered a substantial breeding population of trumpeter swans in Alaska. And in 1957, ninety-two were counted in Grande

Prairie, Alberta, Canada. To increase the population, in the 1960s biologists introduced trumpeters into the Lacreek National Wildlife Refuge in South Dakota and Hennepin Parks in Minnesota. There were more reintroductions (although none on the Atlantic coast) and numbers gradually increased. By the 1980s extinction was no longer dangerously close. In the summer of 2000 biologists counted more than 23,000 trumpeters in North America. Most of them were in Alaska with only 6,500 in the continental United States and Canada.

Even though trumpeter swans were back in some of their former range, biologists still faced a challenge. They wanted to reintroduce trumpeters to eastern North America too, but only as a migrating population. Although Alaskan swans and those from Alberta, Canada, knew migration routes, all the reintroductions had been nonmigratory. Until Bill Lishman, no one had ever tried to teach birds migration routes.

Migration is important. In an ecosystem all plants, animals, and microbes depend on one another, fitting together like the parts of a bicycle. With a part missing, the system is unbalanced. A non-native species entering the gap causes even more disruption.

Take mute swans, for instance. Mutes are natives of Europe and Asia. People who admired these swans brought them to North America in 1889, keeping them captive on private ponds. However, in 1962, during a fierce storm with high tides, five mute swans escaped from their pond into the Chesapeake Bay. Those five multiplied like dandelions. Now there are nearly 4,500 mute swans on the bay. Mutes stay in one place year-round, claiming the best nesting spots. When migratory ducks and geese arrive, the aggressive mutes drive them away. Trumpeter swans, on the other hand, are more tolerant. They often allow smaller waterfowl, especially ducks, to live in their nesting territories, which can be large enough to include a whole pond or lake.

Swans, like sheep, feed by grazing. Before sheep can nibble the grass blades down to

ABOVE: *In 1892 the four- to five-inch-long trumpeter swan eggs were so valued, they sold for four dollars each, while a loaf of bread cost just five cents.* © Jeff Foott/Bruce Coleman Inc.

17

the dirt, the farmer moves them to another pasture so the grass can grow back. But there is no farmer to move the mute swans, and they have no desire to migrate. They eat the underwater vegetation—what scientists call "SAV," or submerged aquatic vegetation—year-round, depleting the supply. Migrating trumpeters ate SAV too, but they flew to their nesting grounds for the spring and summer, allowing the SAV to grow back.

Gavin says, "We see the imbalance caused by the sedentary mute swans and see the resulting problems. We should try to get all ecosystems back to normal balance. Saving trumpeters is one important step toward saving the whole wetland ecosystem. Trumpeters are good ambassadors for wetlands. People can't help noticing such majestic, beautiful birds. The Atlantic Flyway Council wants to reintroduce trumpeter swans to the East Coast, but only if they will be migratory—to maintain ecological balance. So we have to prove that we can teach the swans to migrate."

Only recently have scientists realized the necessity of migration. The reintroductions have resulted in sedentary birds, since left on their own, swans are very slow to establish migration routes. Only a very small number of birds in the reintroduction projects have had the courage to migrate.

Swans from one of these reintroductions—Wye Marsh in Canada—have established a short migration route. Pigpen discovered it. (Pigpen's name? When she was a fuzzy cygnet, Pigpen always had food smeared over her face. *Pen* is the name for a female swan—a male is a *cob*.) Michelle Hudolin, previously the swan keeper at Wye Marsh, says, "Pigpen first flew to Burlington Bay near Toronto in the early '90s. In spite of being blind in one eye and eleven years old now, she has migrated every year except one, when her wing was injured. And most important, she takes her mate, her offspring of several years, and other swans with her. It doesn't sound very exciting when you tell people that they go to the north

OPPOSITE: *By the early 1900s, mute swans had escaped captivity in the Hudson River Valley and spread to Cape Cod. Later, others escaped into the Chesapeake Bay.*

ABOVE: *Before the early 1800s, if you wanted to write a letter, a quill pen was your only choice. Even with steel pens available, John James Audubon, the famous early-American bird artist, used a trumpeter swan quill for his most delicate drawing.*

shore of Lake Ontario, it's so close [one hundred miles as the swan flies]. But when you consider that they have lost the knowledge of their migration routes, it's significant."

Other Wye Marsh trumpeters have wandered—one even flew to West Virginia—but they've never returned to the same wintering spot, so no migration route was established. Michelle says, "Swans tend to be slow to colonize new areas since they are so cautious."

Gavin feels that "left on their own to find the way, trumpeters may take many generations over many years to again find their safest and best wintering areas." That's why he wants to lead the trumpeters to a good wintering area—the Chesapeake Bay.

Growing Up

OPPOSITE: *A trumpeter prepares to turn its eggs, which are concealed down in the nest.*
RIGHT: *An automated incubator turns the eggs.* © Gavin G. Shire

The birds that Gavin was training in the second year of the Trumpeter Swan Migration Project were hatched from eggs that he and his team collected from nests of captive swans.

After collection, the eggs were kept warm by an incubator instead of by a swan mother. The automated incubator tilted the eggs one way and then another, just as a nesting swan turns the eggs in the wild. Why go to all that effort? Turning the egg prevents the membranes that enclose the embryo, the developing swan, from sticking to the shell.

When the eggs hatched in mid-June, Mojo was the first out of the shell. (*Mojo* means "number one" in Swahili, an African language.) Just over an hour old, she clambered among the unhatched eggs of her family, giving them an occasional curious peck. She cheeped constantly. And she could hear the other cygnets cheeping too, from inside their eggs as they broke through. Tough shells. Hard work. Mojo freed herself and dried off in an hour. But some cygnets worked for over a day before they struggled out.

Ducks, geese, and swans are called precocial (pree-COH-shul), hatching with bright eyes, a full coat of fuzzy down, and strong legs. And they can swim—following their parents into open water when only one or two days old. That's where they are safest.

By comparison, most land birds, like robins, hatch blind and weak. Instead of having a soft coat of down, they are naked or nearly so. Birds like this, who need their parents to provide warmth and food, are called altricial (al-TRISH-ul).

Unlike land bird parents, who spend a few weeks cramming food down the gaping bills of their helpless youngsters, swan parents have it easy. They never actually feed their cygnets! At first the little ones eat insects and vegetation near the water surface. Later, parents churn the water with their webbed, clawed feet to wash mud away from roots growing on the bottom. Then with a flip they stand on their heads, feet bicycling for balance, as they dig and pull with their bills. The plants float to the surface, and the little ones dine on salad. The UltraSwans' parents—Gavin and biologists Stephanie Scholarie and Michelle O'Malley—didn't stand on their heads in a pond to dig food for their cygnets. Instead they picked clover and dipped into bags of zoo pellets.

You have probably seen fuzzy ducklings following their mother as if attached with invisible strings. In a process called "imprinting," ducklings, goslings, and cygnets adopt the first moving things they see as "Mom and Dad," following them faithfully. The UltraSwans adopted Gavin, Stephanie, and Michelle as parents.

Little swans also follow their parents' voices—voices already memorized through the walls of the eggshell. Since the biologists wanted the cygnets to follow the trike, they played a tape of the trike motor during the long hours of hatching.

When only a few days old, the cygnets followed the wingless trike for a very short walk as one of the biologists taxied it on the ground. When old enough to walk from their

OPPOSITE, LEFT: *Mojo hatched first. The rest of her family are busy pipping (punching) holes around their shells. They use an egg tooth powered by a hatching muscle on the neck. (The tiny sharp pick at the tip of Mojo's bill is her egg tooth.) A few days after a cygnet hatches, the egg tooth falls off and the hatching muscle gradually disappears.* © Gavin G. Shire

OPPOSITE, RIGHT: *A swan tips up to pull plants.*

pen to the pond, the swans followed the trike on land; on water they followed a yellow boat outfitted with a boombox playing the trike tape. For the next step, Gavin taxied the trike faster and faster until the cygnets found themselves running. In late September, with the wing added to the aircraft, Gavin led the UltraSwans into the air.

The previous year, Gavin had led three swans behind his ultralight the 103 miles from their training site at Airlie, Virginia, to the Chesapeake Bay. That was in December. The next spring one swan returned to just 18 miles away from home. The second was on the way, but when she landed in a neighborhood she was injured by an attacking rottweiler dog. And the third flew more than half of the return route before a storm turned her back to the bay. The scientists were delighted! They had proved that trumpeters could be taught to migrate behind an ultralight.

For this, the second year, Gavin wanted to fly a migration route that trumpeter swans had used in the past. He found it when Dan Carroll, a biologist with the New York State Department of Conservation (NYSDEC), learned of the Trumpeter Swan Migration Project. After seeing the damaging effect mute swans can have on the ecosystem, Dan too wanted to restore native trumpeters. He managed a NYSDEC area in western New York where trumpeters lived hundreds of years ago. It would be a great place for the swans' summer home. The area included a large farm. A flat field with lots of open space around it could serve as an airstrip. There was a pond for the afternoon swim. A national wildlife refuge and an Indian reservation were nearby. All three areas had numerous marshy ponds—good habitat for swans returning the next spring. The farm fit the bill. On September 16, the biologists and "year two" cygnets, now three months old, moved from Virginia to western New York.

Gavin planned migration for late November, hoping to leave before snow and wind grounded the ultralight. That gave the cygnets a little over two months to strengthen the muscles they would need to fly 320 miles—when they would be only five and a half months old!

Preparing for migration, Gavin faced a dilemma. There were nineteen swans in three family groups, but only two pilots and two trikes. Gavin decided to train the strongest fliers in one big group and the weaker fliers in a second group. It seemed like a good idea—two teams, each comprised of swans of equal abilities. But Gavin quickly learned that swans have very strong family bonds. He says, "The birds didn't like each other. Instead of following, they fought in the air." Gavin relented and returned them to their original family groups.

From two of these families Gavin chose swans who followed best. And on December 4, Gavin and Brooke Pennypacker, the other pilot, began migration with a group of five swans behind one trike and a group of four behind the other trike. (Volunteers trucked the remaining ten swans.) Bill Lishman, the first person to migrate with birds, came to help. He brought along pilot Joe Duff, who had helped fly the goose migrations. They were to be the "chase" pilots who rounded up wandering birds.

Just as trikes and swans lifted off, the wind came up, making flying rough. The birds could fly

faster than the trikes, and on two occasions a swan flew above Gavin's ultralight wing and was caught in the wires. Luckily, Gavin knew what to do when that happened—nearly stall the aircraft, just short of letting it fall to the ground. Then the bird could drop out of the wires. But as each bird dropped down, it hit the propeller. One lost a wing and one cut his foot. Veterinarians patched them up, but Gavin was deeply concerned. He knew more injuries or worse lay ahead. It was time to try something different.

Gavin decided to truck all the swans to each stop, where he and Brooke flew them in ten-mile-wide circles up to 2,000 feet high. That was safe, since the planes could climb faster than the birds. From that height, in clear weather, the swans could see the next stop. But, could they put these circles together in a chain and find their way back?

The trumpeters spent the winter on Chesapeake Bay. When spring came they showed the urge to migrate—they wandered—but they didn't return to western New York. So Michelle and volunteers trucked them there for the summer. When winter came, Glory was the first of the swans to realize it was best to head south. He flew as far as southern Pennsylvania, where someone recognized his UltraSwan neckband and called the project office to report his whereabouts. After spending the winter there, the next spring he flew north to New York, landing 50 miles from his starting point. That was a good sign for the scientists!

What about the rest of Glory's flock? They also might have tried to migrate in a day or so, but, sadly, five were illegally shot. (Several hunters' clubs and a local contractor contributed to a reward fund but the offenders haven't been found.) Brooke quickly captured the remaining swans and transported them to Virginia to live in retirement. Gavin couldn't lead these birds on migration again the next fall. Swans past eight months old won't follow an ultralight. So they now swim, along with Glory, on the protected ponds at the research institute.

OPPOSITE, LEFT: *Glory flew to southern Pennsylvania for the winter. He left about January 6 and arrived in Claysburg on January 22, 2000. The next spring, on March 30, he was found fifty miles east of his starting point. Volunteer Doug Domedian caught him with a flying tackle that would make any football coach proud.* OPPOSITE, RIGHT: *UltraSwans spent the winter on the Chesapeake Bay.*

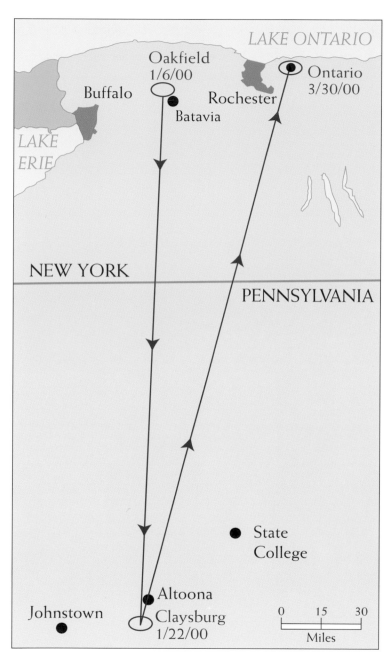

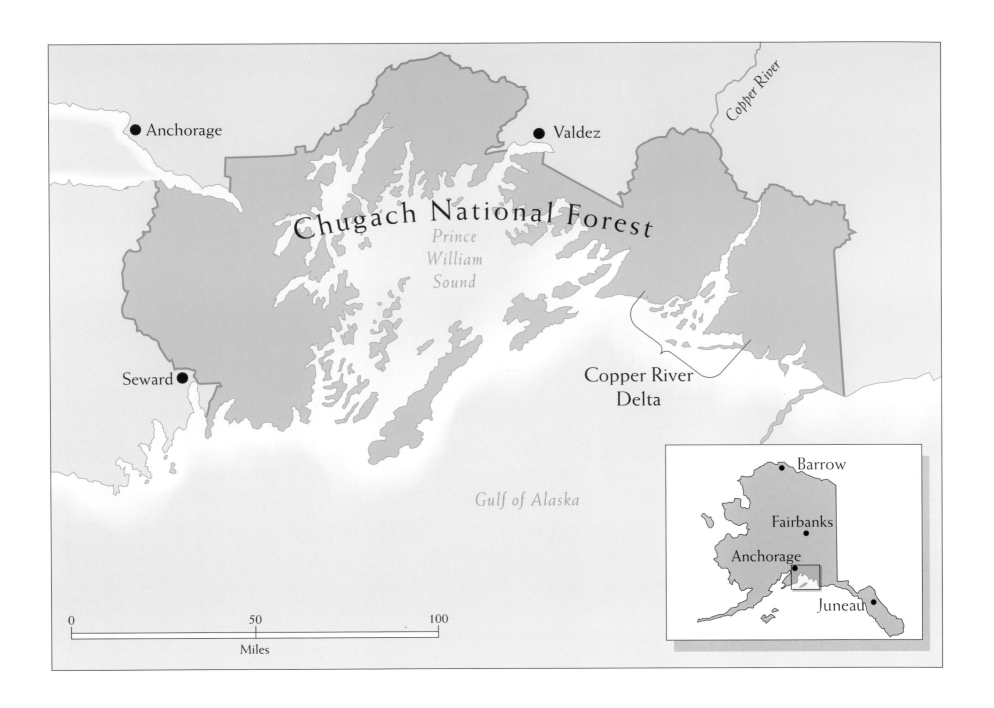

Anchorage

Valdez

Copper River

Chugach National Forest

Prince
William
Sound

Seward

Copper River
Delta

Gulf of Alaska

Barrow

Fairbanks

Anchorage

Juneau

0   50   100

Miles

Year Three—
UltraSwans in Training

OPPOSITE: *Brooke traveled to Alaska and the Chugach National Forest to collect cygnets. National Forest Service people took him to the swans' nesting area in the Copper River Delta.*

During a year off to regroup, Gavin, Stephanie, and Michelle left the project and Brooke became the team leader for the third experiment. Brooke was eager to build on what they all had learned from previous years.

After Gavin's experiment, Brooke knew that groups must be made up of families and not a mix. He said, "This year we are standing on Gavin's shoulders and his previous work. Science is a compilation of effort and sacrifice. Each person comes up with a little piece of the puzzle and it builds up. There are no failures in science if you learn from each try. You never learn everything. It's ongoing."

This time Brooke wanted to keep the trumpeter swans wilder. The year one and year two flocks, who imprinted on humans, were too trusting for their own good. Brooke knew that Wayne Bezner Kerr, a Canadian scientist, had done a study to see which swans followed better—those imprinted on humans or those imprinted on swans. Wayne left one group of cygnets with their own swan parents for ten days, long enough for imprinting to take place, and he imprinted another group on humans. When he led each group behind his ultralight, he found that the birds imprinted on swans followed better. So Brooke

LEFT, TOP: *The team that helped Brooke (far right) collect cygnets in Alaska.* © Brooke Pennypacker

LEFT, BOTTOM: *The airboat is ready to travel to the swans.* © Brooke Pennypacker

adopted a new plan. He would let wild trumpeter swan parents hatch the cygnets this time—no more eggs from captive swans and no more incubators.

In late June, Brooke went to Alaska to collect ten-day-old cygnets. U.S. Forest Service people had found trumpeter swan nests in a remote area of the Copper River Delta. They and a U.S. Geological Survey team took Brooke in on a noisy airboat as far as it could go. Then, while hungry insects lunched on them, they canoed and waded in rain and cold the rest of the way to the nests.

The wild trumpeters wanted no part of humans. Except for one who defended her cygnets, all the other swans flew away. The cygnets, too young to fly, instinctively dived under the water for safety. But Brooke knew a trick. He followed a diving bird in his canoe. When the cygnet came up the third time, almost out of air, he leaned over and grabbed it out of the water.

For the flight to Airlie, Virginia, Brooke put the cygnets in dog crates with nonslip flooring. A leg sliding out from under a swan's heavy body can cause the ankle tendon to slip out of place, rendering the leg useless. That is a fatal injury for a swan, since there is no remedy. (Fortunately, this rarely happens in the wild.) Brooke had asked experts what to use for flooring in the boxes. All except one said, "It won't work." But that one told Brooke, "I think geotextile matting is the answer, and I'll find out what brand will be best." He was right—the cygnets arrived with tendons in place.

To keep the swans afraid of humans and as wild as possible, the project team decided to hide "good" humans. Anyone who gave the swans things they liked—food, water, and flying—would be hidden in a uniform. For things the swans didn't like—health checks and herding them into their pens—people would wear ordinary clothes.

Brooke designed the new uniform. He wasn't convinced that trumpeter swans could see color, so he chose a uniform of high contrast—a black suit with broad white stripes. A red face mask, red goggles, and a black helmet covered the head. Black gloves and black boots covered hands and feet. The identity of the person inside was concealed.

A research assistant, Kyra Hawn, while wearing the uniform, taught the cygnets to follow. She said, "It was like walking my dog twice a day. Only I took my boombox." The boombox played a loud tape recording of the trike motor. First the trumpeters followed for five feet and Kyra gave them a reward of food. Then they followed ten feet

ABOVE: *Walt Sturgeon, a swan expert, helped Brooke with the Alaskan cygnets.* © Brooke Pennypacker

ABOVE: *Brooke puts on the uniform he designed.*

for their reward. Still uniformed, she paddled a boat while they followed. Next, Brooke, also in uniform, led them behind his wingless trike as he taxied it. To encourage them to follow, he squawked a bicycle horn, which sounded something like a parent trumpeter.

By the end of September the UltraSwans were fledging—flight feathers were replacing the pale gray down. For identification, the birds wore colored neckbands. The bottom color indicated the family group; the top color, the individual. Santa, named for his red and green neckband, flapped his wings as he ran after the taxiing ultralight. Suddenly he was in the air, at least three feet off the ground. After fifteen feet of clumsy flying, barely missing a tree, he landed, looked surprised, and turned to see if anyone else in his family had flown. No! He stretched his neck, bobbed up and down, and had a lot to "say," he was so excited. Flying for a big bird is as challenging as learning to ride a bicycle without training wheels. Kyra often saw the trumpeters do face plants as they attempted to land.

The fourteen fledglings were gaining skill in the air—flying higher and faster. Soon they would be above the treetops. Scientists think trumpeters migrate back to the place where they first flew high enough to see the surrounding landscape. Brooke wanted them to see western New York, not Virginia. So in early October a caravan of vehicles made the

long day's drive north to Dan Carroll's NYSDEC farm. Even though the temperature was in the forties, Brooke opened the windows in his van and turned the air conditioning on as well! He wanted to be sure the six Alaskan swans in dog crates in the back didn't overheat.

The community was thrilled to have swans back again. A number of people volunteered their help—Laurie Kramer worked in the office and cared for the swans, others handled publicity, maintained the airstrip, and chased UltraSwans out of off-limits ponds. A call came from Mark Reese, a Vermont ultralight pilot. He said, "Would you like me to help fly? I can spare some time from my carpentry business."

As training progressed, people on their way to work early in the morning stopped by to climb the small viewing hill. Watching the trumpeters fly with the ultralight, one woman said, "This is exciting. These swans were gone. It's really special to be bringing them back." Another said, "It must be cool as heck to have birds flying with you."

Sometimes when Brooke looked down from the air, he saw cars stop in the middle of the road. No one was used to seeing birds this big, let alone birds and an ultralight flying together.

Every day after the morning flight, the team moved the four living-room-sized swan pens to clean spots on the field next to the airstrip. Kyra learned to drive a tractor and trailer to bring a large water tank along with clean wading pools each day. As she filled the pools, she sprayed the swans with the hose. They loved to bite at the spray and splash in it. She also refilled their grit pans. Why feed the birds sand? Swans have no teeth to grind their food. Instead, sand grinds it for them in a special organ called the gizzard.

Next Kyra took food into the pens. Kyra didn't talk to the swans. She didn't want them to connect her with humans. Out of curiosity the birds pulled at her uniform and pecked on her helmet.

As she fed them, Kyra heard the swans constantly "talking." As the high cheeps of fuzzy cygnets changed to the medium-range, gentle "*unnhks, unnhks*" of juveniles, a voice

ABOVE: *Young people can help too. Brooke's eight-year-old son, Devin, helped clean wading pools while the swans were in Virginia.*

OPPOSITE, TOP: *Before sunup, Brooke and Mark put the ultralight together.*

OPPOSITE, BOTTOM: *Young swans scramble out of their pen to follow Brooke into the air.*

sometimes cracked just like a human teenager's. They moaned too, and Santa moaned especially loud. June, in the white family, had a call that sounded so much like a person saying "Hel-lo" that volunteers would look to see who was there. When they heard the trike motor, all of the swans turned up the volume, giving loud, excited *"onhk, onhk"* calls. One man watching a training flight said, "It sounds like my ten-year-old son learning the trumpet, trying to get out the first few notes." Adult swans trumpet a *"ko-hoh"* that sounds like a diesel truck horn and is so loud it can carry for over a mile. The Latin name for trumpeter swans, *Cygnus buccinator*, does not describe a trumpet, however. *Cygnus* means "swan" and *buccinator* is derived from *buccina*, the word for an ancient Roman trombone.

Brooke used a slow trike to begin flight training. As the UltraSwans developed strength and flew faster, he used a faster wing, then a faster trike. Remembering from Gavin's experiment that birds flying in front of the trike risked injury, Brooke wanted to fly fast enough to stay in the lead.

While Brooke flew one family, Mark, the volunteer pilot, taught the other families to accept each

LEFT, TOP: *Brooke placed the pens next to the airstrip so the swans could run right out the door for takeoff.*

LEFT, BOTTOM: *Kyra drives the water tank and clean wading pools to the pens.*

OPPOSITE, TOP: *Wearing her uniform, Kyra feeds the swans.*

OPPOSITE, BOTTOM: *Kyra pours sand into the grit pans.*

new trike with its different-sounding motor, different color, and different shape. He got into uniform, taxied the new trike past the pens, honked the bicycle horn, and fed the birds.

Mark was an experienced pilot and instructor, but he needed Brooke's lessons in flying with birds. In early November Mark was ready to help train the swans to fly higher and faster. Mountains lay ahead.

On one of the few evenings with wind calm enough, Brooke wanted to take the swans on a training flight. But engine trouble with the trike delayed him. The sun went down after only twenty minutes of flying. Brooke was forced to land, as aviation rules don't allow ultralights to fly after dark. The birds weren't tired; they were used to flying longer—for more than an hour. In the pink and gold sky they circled and circled, eyeing a distant, wonderful-looking pond. The temptation was too much. A volunteer chased after them in his all-terrain vehicle (ATV). Yelling and waving his arms, he startled them out of the water. The swans flew toward the airfield—until his back was turned. Then they headed for the pond again. This time the volunteer even waded into the water to chase the wayward birds out, but they cir-

OPPOSITE: *In late October, Brooke takes the trumpeters up for a rare evening training flight. Most evenings had been too windy.*

cled right back. The volunteer gave up, climbed on his ATV, and endured a cold ride back in soaking wet clothes. Meanwhile, Kyra stood on the airstrip honking the bicycle horn. Finally, when it was pitch dark, the swans flew back and Kyra locked them in their pens.

On another training flight, a swan named Trinity caught her wing in the ultralight propeller. Fortunately she was not injured, but some feathers were cut off. The next day, when let out to fly with the trike, she couldn't get off the ground. As Kyra shut her into her pen, she kicked the door. She wanted to fly!

Dr. Glenn Olsen, a veterinarian, offered to try to fix Trinity's wing. When he came to do physicals, required by the state of Maryland before the swans could be released into the Chesapeake Bay, he weighed all the swans and took blood and fecal samples. Then he was ready to repair the damaged wing.

He knew how falconers (people licensed to keep falcons and hawks in captivity) fixed a broken flight feather. They had done it for thousands of years using a wooden dowel to fasten the broken end of the feather to a replacement feather. No one had ever tried to fix a swan's feather. Wood was too weak for such a large bird. Glenn decided to try a stainless steel welding rod. He neatly clipped off the broken part of Trinity's feather, leaving the good section. From a replacement feather that he brought, he cut the correct length to replace the broken part. (The replacements came from captive swans who already had some of their feathers clipped short to prevent flying. Glenn said, "They won't miss a few flight feathers.") Next, with a hand drill, he hollowed out both feather shafts. Neither the clipping nor the drilling hurt—no more than a haircut hurts you. Glenn filled both shafts with strong glue and inserted the welding rod in each, pulling the cut end of the replacement feather against the clipped end of the broken feather. But the glue failed to dry. It was too cold in the unheated garage. Laurie, one of the volunteers, found a hair dryer to set the glue. Soon,

Trinity's five broken feathers looked as good as new—except for a sharp line where the new feathers met her original ones. When the ultralight flew again, Trinity flew with it.

The birds were nearly strong enough for migration. They had put in many flight training days due to exceptionally good weather—clear and calm. That is, until November 14. Strong winds blew in that day. Six days later, snow came too. Brooke and Kyra drove their jeep the half-mile from the farmhouse to the pens. But on the way back the snow came down so hard and thick that they couldn't see any landmarks through the white. The next day two feet of snow buried the airstrip. Their jeep couldn't handle snow that deep, so a volunteer drove Kyra and Laurie to the pens—in a front-end loader. Wild swans would have started south when snow and ice covered their food. But the ultralights couldn't fly until calm weather returned.

Windy, snowy weather continued. Brooke was concerned. It was past time for migration. So even though December 19 was a snowy day, he started out with the swans. With very few training days since mid-November, the trumpeters had lost strength and some dropped out. After circling the airfield a few times, Brooke decided the swans weren't ready. On December 29, the team chose the eight strongest fliers and started off again. That day didn't prove to be any better. The weather again was snowy, with temperatures in the teens. The pilots felt frozen, three of the birds dropped out, and one bird was killed when it collided with the ultralight. Brooke knew the weather conditions were too dangerous for both pilots and swans. The team crated the birds and returned to the farm, where Brooke changed plans. He decided to truck the whole project to the middle of Pennsylvania, where the weather would be better. He would continue migration from there.

OPPOSITE, TOP LEFT: *Glenn inserts a welding rod, which has a replacement feather glued over one end, into the prepared broken feather shaft.*

OPPOSITE, BOTTOM LEFT: *Trinity's five imped feathers will lift her into the air again. Imped is a word falconers use to mean restored feathers.*

OPPOSITE, RIGHT: *Laurie* (left) *and Kyra* (right), *engulfed in snow, fix the electric fence, which repels predators.*

To the Bay!

A meteorologist in the Buffalo, New York, weather office told Brooke, "The weather looks good in Pennsylvania for the next few days." So on January 11, the team folded pens and ultralight wings, loaded trikes and gear onto a trailer, crated the UltraSwans, and drove to Pennsylvania.

The next morning Brooke and Mark flew the birds to test their strength after so much time off. The pilots carefully watched the swans' breathing. When they saw a bird gasp for air after every third wing beat, they knew the swan was too tired to keep going. Brooke radioed back to Laurie, "How long has my group been up?" Laurie checked her stopwatch and answered, "Twenty-eight minutes." The pilots must land before the swans become too tired and drop to the ground anyplace. It's difficult collecting them, and it's bad for training if they learn they can leave the ultralight. Brooke decided that five of the birds were strong enough to fly the next day.

That evening the temperature dropped well below freezing. Ethan, with a white and green neckband, slept in his wading pool, feet dangling in the icy slush. Other swans preened and "talked" in their contented voices, "*unnhk, unnhk.*"

LEFT, TOP: *Thick mittens keep Mark's hands warm.*

LEFT, BOTTOM: *Mark used a pencil to push the buttons on the GPS.*

OPPOSITE, TOP: *Brooke adjusts the trike motor before takeoff.*

OPPOSITE, BOTTOM: *After every flight, the swans enjoy their pools.*

Mark strung electric wire along the outside of the pens to keep predators out. He said, "This will get the attention of anyone who comes along and touches a wet nose to it." (It wouldn't injure the predator, just give it a jolting shock.)

On January 13, in Numidia, Pennsylvania, the UltraSwan migration continued. The rising sun gave the frosty air a white glow that almost hid the snowy fields and forests. Under their uniforms Brooke and Mark wore electric vests crisscrossed with battery-powered heating wires. Mark pulled on big mittens with hand-warmers inside. Instead of his fingers he used a pencil, tied on with string, to punch the buttons on his GPS (global positioning system). Brooke wore goggles but Mark insisted on wearing a bubble face helmet after suffering a frostbitten nose during training. Last, they strapped clipboards holding maps to their legs. Mostly though, the pilots relied on a GPS to direct them on their route to the Chesapeake Bay.

Brooke took off with two red group females, Grace and Kate. As Brooke circled to gain altitude, Grace, red/red, lagged behind. Brooke's voice came on the radio, "I'm bringing them back. Red/red is gasping. She can't get high enough to cross these mountains." After they landed, Laurie herded Grace into her pen. Then Brooke took off again with Kate, red/black. A few minutes later, Mark led the green group of three birds into the air. They circled in front of the moon, still visible in spite of the bright morning sun. The buzz of Mark's motor faded as ultralight and birds disappeared over the mountain.

Volunteers scurried to dismantle the remaining pens and pack them into a trailer along with all the buckets, hoses, pools, and other gear. The birds who weren't strong enough to migrate had been put in dog crates earlier and were already riding in vans to the next stop. The drivers wound along country roads, knowing the straight-flying ultralights and swans would arrive ahead of them. They wondered—had the pilots and birds landed safely? Yes. Brooke and Mark were discussing their flight and the UltraSwans were all in their pens, eating corn or happily splashing in their pools.

In the afternoon Brooke and Mark flew the nonmigrators so they could get a swan's-eye view of

the area. If they followed the migrators back next spring, at least they would know part of the route.

After waiting out a few days of wind, the birds flew another successful trip. But a storm was predicted soon and there were two more legs to go. The next morning, even though an iron-gray overcast sky looked ominous, Brooke decided the wind was calm enough to fly. Brooke said, "Clear prop" to warn everyone to stay clear of the propeller as he started his trike motor. He took off with Grace, red/red, and her sister, Kate. He radioed back, "Grace is doing fine today."

Erin, green/black, in the green family pen, heard the trike motor. "*Onhking*" loudly, he pushed the pen door with his big foot, then jumped as high

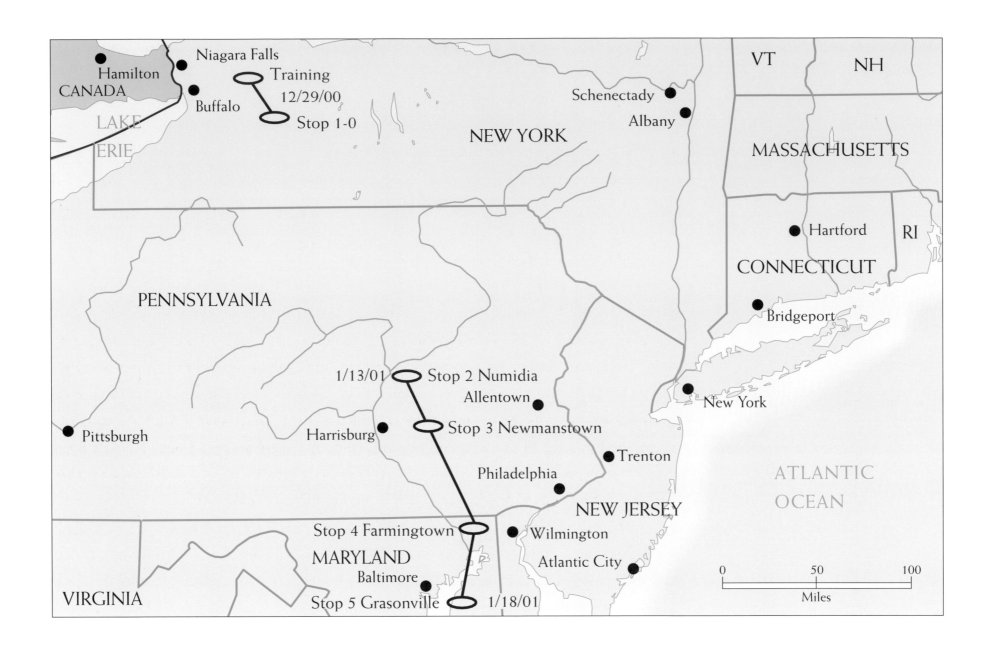

Niagara Falls
Hamilton
CANADA
Buffalo
LAKE
ERIE
Training
12/29/00
Stop 1-0

NEW YORK

Schenectady
Albany

VT
NH

MASSACHUSETTS

Hartford
RI

CONNECTICUT

PENNSYLVANIA

Bridgeport

1/13/01 Stop 2 Numidia
Allentown

New York

Pittsburgh

Harrisburg Stop 3 Newmanstown

Trenton

Philadelphia

NEW JERSEY

Stop 4 Farmingtown
MARYLAND Wilmington
Baltimore Atlantic City

VIRGINIA Stop 5 Grasonville 1/18/01

ATLANTIC
OCEAN

0   50   100

Miles

OPPOSITE: *In December, the pilots led the swans on the first leg of migration in New York State. In January they continued on in Pennsylvania.*

as he could. He wanted to fly too! Minutes later Mark taxied up and Laurie yanked the green family's pen door away. Up in the air, Mark radioed, "My three birds are flying well."

Then came a message from Brooke, "The cloud ceiling is lowering. Visibility is getting poor." After flying a few miles more, he said, "The weather is better now and the swans are still flying well. We are going to skip the next stop and go all the way to the bay." Later, in his headset, Mark heard Brooke say, "There is a little freezing rain now, but it won't be a problem." Both pilots knew that as ice builds up on the ultralight wing, it changes the wing's shape, causing the plane to lose lift. Mark was concerned about flying into freezing rain, and he was quite relieved when it soon stopped.

Swans and pilots face dangers besides ice. One leg of migration took them over vast expanses of forest. Pilots are uneasy without an emergency landing site in view. Ultralights can't land in treetops. Neither can heavy trumpeter swans. Other aircraft are a danger as well. Turbulence from a helicopter can slam an ultralight to the ground. When an army helicopter cut in front of Mark south of Numidia, he had a few anxious moments before he knew he was safe. As for swans—they can hit the plane. Mark says, "You have to know where the birds are all the time and be ready to dodge every second. I need an owl's head so I can turn to see directly behind me. It's nerve-wracking and hard work. At the same time, it's a thrill to have them flying off the wingtip looking at me."

Mark faced another challenge in the air—his plane kept turning left. He looked up at the right wing, and saw the problem. With his bill Erin was holding on to one of the two-inch-long bungee cords protruding from the back of the wing. He had cupped his wings into a glide position, and was enjoying a free ride. Erin's seven feet of added wing was

turning the plane! Using his control bar, Mark leveled the wing, but Erin grabbed hold again—three times. Finally Erin realized a free ride was hopeless. After landing, Mark said, "I must be the world's first swan tow pilot."

Before reaching their destination, the pilots had to fly a straight course over the water of the bay. Pilots don't like flying over water any more than flying over forest. Mark says, "A two-stroke engine, like the ultralight uses, is about a thousand times more unreliable than a jet engine. If the engine quits, you go kerplunk."

But the swans thought it was the best scenery yet. Their heads twisted and turned as they looked at the water far below. At nine-thirty A.M. on January 18, after an hour and a half in the air, they landed at the Wildfowl Trust of North America. At least the ultralights did. The birds kept circling. The Chesapeake Bay off the end of the airstrip proved too enticing. Most of the swans landed right in the water. Brooke took off again, collecting swans behind him as he circled low. He led them to a landing by their pens, where Laurie locked them in.

The next day, Donielle Rininger, lead biologist for the project, brought new collars for the UltraSwans to wear. Even though the swans would be free in the Chesapeake Bay— with many miles of water—Brooke wouldn't lose them. The new yellow collars, numbered this time, included radio transmitters.

ABOVE: *Donielle pulls a new collar over a swan's head. A radio transmitter protrudes from the collar.*
OPPOSITE, TOP: *Mark herds the swans to freedom.*
OPPOSITE, BOTTOM: *Swans love water!*

Release day was set for Saturday, January 20. Dr. William Sladen, the UltraSwan project director, Donielle, people from the Wildfowl Trust (who were helping to look after the swans for the winter), volunteers, and newspaper reporters all came. At ten A.M. Mark opened the first pen. The birds, expecting the usual daily routine, walked slowly as Mark circled behind them, herding them out the door. Then they saw water lapping at the beach eight feet ahead. Water! What every swan loves! Walking accelerated to a mad dash. They called louder than ever. They ran on the water. They took off from the water and landed back in the water—a real pleasure after using a runway of hard ground. They bathed and swam about. When they'd had enough fun, they came ashore to preen with their contented *"unnhk, unnhks."* It was a perfect winter home.

Now it was all up to the swans. Would they find their way back to Pennsylvania after a few months, remembering the map in reverse? Would they teach their future offspring the migration route?

Gavin explains, "This experiment will take up to five more years of raising and training new genera-

tions. And it will take ten years before we know if our goal of reintroducing a migratory population of trumpeter swans to the eastern United States can be reached. The past few years were just the start. But it has been worthwhile. We have learned a lot. Success will come only if each generation teaches the migration route to the next generation. It's obvious from our work that there are many questions still to be answered."

Even though it will take years to establish a migrating population of trumpeter swans in the East, the scientists' strong desire to have a whole environment again spurs them on.

Everyone working with the swans hopes that someday we will again see the majestic white birds winging their way through the sky on their annual migrations.

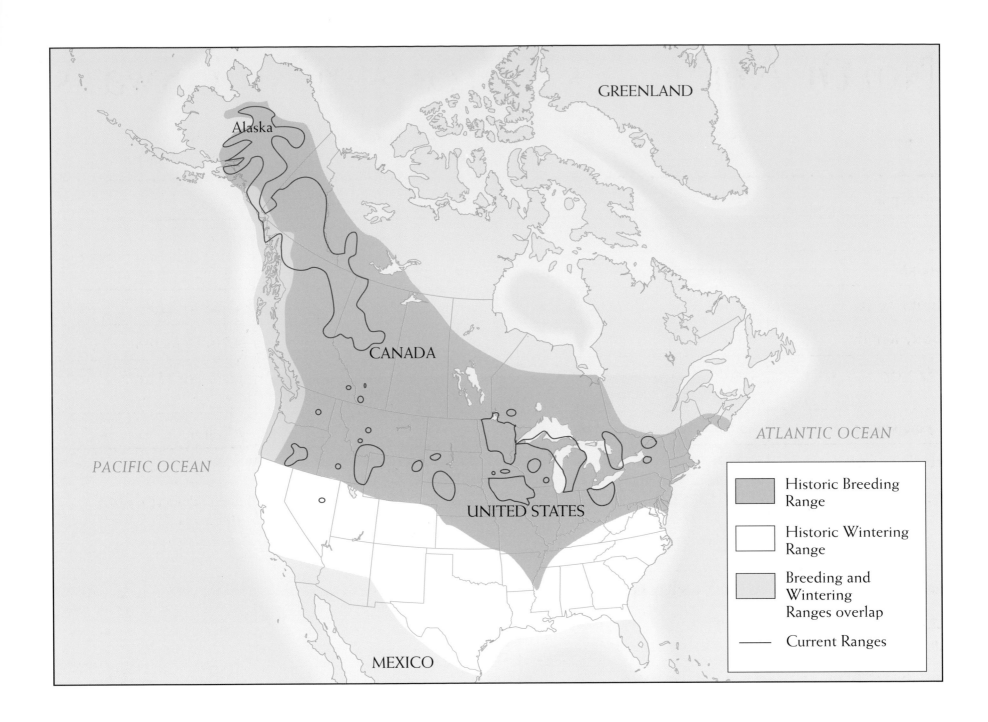

North America's Three Kinds of Swans

	Trumpeter Swan *Cygnus buccinator*	**Mute Swan (introduced)** *Cygnus olor*	**Tundra Swan** *Cygnus columbianus*
wingspan	7 to 8 feet	7 to 8 feet	5.5 to 7 feet
height	up to 4 feet	up to 4 feet	up to 3 feet
weight	20 to 38 pounds	13.4 to 31 pounds	10.5 to 18.6 pounds
foot length	about 5 to 7 inches	about 5 to 7 inches	about 5 inches
body length	55 to 62 inches	56 to 60 inches	47 to 58 inches
life span	record of 24 years in the wild, 32.5 years in captivity	record of 26 years in the wild, 50 years in captivity	record of 25 years in the wild
flying speed	45 to 50 mph, can reach 60 mph	50 mph	51 mph
can breed at	3 or 4 years old	2 or 3 years old	2 or 3 years old
nesting territory	from 4 acres up to 247 acres	there can be a very small territory, with nests adjacent to each other (called "colonial nesting"), or a territory of up to 12 acres	from 58 acres up to 494 acres
nest size	3.9 to 11.8 feet in diameter	averages about 5 feet in diameter	.8 to 1.6 feet in diameter
clutch size (number of eggs laid)	1 to 9	4 to 8	2 to 7
number of feathers	no one has counted trumpeter swan feathers	no one has counted mute swan feathers	25,216

How to tell the three swans apart:

The trumpeter swan has a straight black bill. "Red lipstick" lines it.

The mute swan has a black knob on an orange bill.

The tundra swan has a slightly upcurved black bill with a yellow mark in front of the eye. A tundra can show red lipstick, too. Tundra swans are smallest of the three.

For more information on trumpeter swans: The Trumpeter Swan Society, 3800 County Road 24, Maple Plain, MN 55359. (763) 476-4663, www.taiga.net/swans/index.html.

For more information on the UltraSwans visit the Web site of **Environmental Studies at Airlie,** www.trumpeterswans.org.

Where to see trumpeter swans (selected sites):

Comox Valley Trumpeter Swan Festival
Trumpeter Swan Sentinel Society (TSSS)
Courtenay, BC V9N 2L5
Canada
(250) 334-3234

Crane Creek State Park
Magee Marsh Wildlife Area
13531 West State Route 2
Oak Harbor, OH 43449
(419) 898-2495

Crex Meadows Wildlife Area
P.O. Box 367
Grantsburg, WI 54840
(715) 463-2896
www.crexmeadows.org
www.dnr.state.wi.us/org/land/wildlife/publ/
watchwil/viewguid/crexprev.htm

Environmental Studies at Airlie
captive swans, tours by appointment only
7078 Airlie Road
Warrenton, VA 20187
(888) 264-4728
www.trumpeterswans.org

Hennepin Parks
3800 County Road 24
Maple Plain, MN 55359
(763) 476-4663
www.hennepinparks.org/nrm/wildlife_wildlife
_swanlocations.cfm

Lacreek National Wildlife Refuge
Winter is the best viewing.
HC 5 Box 14
Martin, SD 57551
(605) 685-6508
www.travelsd.com/partners/usfish/usfish.htm
www.wildernet.com

M'Clintock Bay Wildlife Viewing Program
early April to early May
Department of Renewable Resources
Government of Yukon
Box 2703
Whitehorse, Yukon Territory Y1A 2C6
Canada
(867) 667-8291
www.renres.gov.yk.ca/viewtrav/shcos.html

Red Rocks Lakes National Wildlife Refuge
27820 Southside Centennial Road
Lima, MT 59739
(406) 276-3536
www.r6.fws.gov/redrocks/index.html
www.learner.org/jnorth

The Wildfowl Trust of North America
captive swans
Horsehead Wetlands Center
P.O. Box 519
Grasonville, MD 21638
(410) 827-6694
www.wildfowltrust.org

The Wye Marsh Wildlife Centre
Box 100, Hwy 12
Midland, ON L4R4K6
Canada
(705) 526-7809
www.wyemarsh.com

Yellowstone National Park
P.O. Box 168
Yellowstone National Park, WY 82190-0168
Visitor Information - (307) 344-7381
www.nps.gov/yell

Acknowledgments

It was a joy to watch the swans and wonderful getting to know the team and the many volunteers. Besides those volunteers mentioned in the story, there were Dave and Donna Houchin, Don Schmigel, Jim Beaver, Dr. Richard Thoma, Dick Walker, Mike Levins, the Hursts, and Doug Domedion, who waded into the pond to chase truant birds home. There's one more volunteer, whom I already knew, George Osborn, my husband. His help through the whole project was indispensable.

I'm extremely grateful to Gavin Shire and Brooke Pennypacker for making this book possible and for their help all along the way. Gavin spent hours at his dining room table answering my questions, choosing pictures, and reading the manuscript.

Many people helped: all the team members; Dan Carroll and Sonny Knowlton of NYSDEC; Chris Snow of the Wildfowl Trust of North America, who knew where I could find swan tracks; and the Wye Marsh swan keepers, Michelle Hudolin and her successor, Angela Coxon. Michelle and Angela know most of the eighty-plus swans at Wye Marsh by sight! Madeleine Linck of The Trumpeter Swan Society gave me lots of information. Thanks to all!

Also, many thanks to Anita Silvey for her unfailing encouragement, which pointed me in a new direction, and to Amy Flynn, my editor, for her gentle guidance.

I'm grateful to the Genesee Country Village & Museum (www.gcv.org) in Mumford, New York, for the use of their historical office for the quill pen photo.

Lastly, thanks to Dr. Bill Sladen for reading the manuscript and for making this adventure possible by inviting me to go on migration—an experience I'll never forget.

OPPOSITE: *Mark points at the bungee cord that gave Erin the free ride.*

If you would like to give a tax-deductible contribution to the Trumpeter Swan Migration Project, please send a check to:

The International Academy for Preventive Medicine
7078 Airlie Road
Warrenton, VA 20187
Attention: Environmental Studies

Index